MASTERWORKS
OF
CHILDREN'S
LITERATURE

MASTERWORKS
OF
CHILDREN'S
LITERATURE

Volume Seven
Victorian
Color Picture
Books

EDITOR *Jonathan Cott*

COMMENTARY BY *Maurice Sendak*

THE STONEHILL PUBLISHING COMPANY
IN ASSOCIATION WITH
CHELSEA HOUSE PUBLISHERS
NEW YORK

GENERAL EDITOR: Jonathan Cott
VOLUME EDITOR: Jonathan Cott

DESIGNER: Paul Bacon
PROJECT DIRECTORS: Esther Mitgang, Heather F. White
PRODUCTION: CoCo Dupuy Spencer, Sandra Su, Wendell Niles

ISBN: 0-87754-381-X
LC: 79-89986

First Printing
Printed in Japan by Dai-Nippon

The Publisher would like to acknowledge with grateful
appreciation the generous permission to reproduce from
the collection of Esther Mitgang the work of R.M. Ballantyne,
which appears as the final chapter in this volume under the title
"The Butterfly's Ball."

Chelsea House Publishers
   Harold Steinberg, Chairman and Publisher
   Andrew E. Norman, President
   Susan Lusk, Vice President
A Division of Chelsea House Educational Communications, Inc.
133 Christopher Street, New York, NY 10014

Dedicated to the Memory of
Jeffrey Joshua Steinberg
Founder and President of
Stonehill Communications, Inc.

Contents

Preface

THE DEVELOPMENT OF illustration in children's books—whose origins go back to bestiaries, rhymed treatises, primers, and the invention of the horn- and chap-book—has a long and fascinating history, one which has been well documented in a number of reference works.* But Gleeson White, in his important *Children's Books and Their Illustrators* (first published as a Special Winter Number of *The Studio* for 1897–98), states that it was not until the beginning of the nineteenth century that children's book illustrations—as we conceive of them today—truly came into their own. Having discovered that "children possessed the right to be amused," White writes, "the imagination of poets and artists addressed itself at last to the most appreciative of audiences, a world of newcomers, with insatiable appetites for wonders real and imaginary."

Clearly, however, the extraordinary work for children by illustrators such as Cruikshank and Doyle attests to the fact that the art of children's book illustration—as it developed and then blossomed in the 1860s and '70s in England—could never be considered as distinct or separate from the magnificent body of work created by illustrators such as Crane, Tenniel, Millais, Hunt, Hughes, Watson, and scores of others—all of whom illustrated *books*, whether for children or adults.† Still, any overall view of English children's literature that neglected to present specific examples of the art of Victorian color picture books not only would be incomplete but would deprive readers of seeing some of the most imaginatively designed and beautiful color printing (as developed and promoted by people like Senefelder, Baxter, Kronheim, and Edmund Evans) ever produced for children.

No one in our own time better exemplifies the Victorian tradition of children's book illustration than Maurice Sendak, whose work—drawing its inspiration as much from Caldecott and Hughes as from Dürer and Runge—expresses the enormous range and power of all significant illustration, whatever its intended audience. More than seventy of Sendak's books for children have been published in the United States and abroad, and his works have been cited on seventeen separate occasions by the *New York Times* as among the best illustrated books of the year. He has been the recipient of scores of awards, among them the 1964 Caldecott Medal, the 1969 *Deutsche Jugendbuchpreis*, the Lewis Carroll Shelf Award—as well as awards from the Library of Congress, the Library Journal, and the American Library Association. He was also the first American to receive the Illustrator's Medal of the Hans Christian Andersen Award in 1970. In 1983, he received the Laura Ingalls Wilder Award. He has recently turned to the designing of costumes and sets for operas such as Mozart's *The Magic Flute*, Janáček's *The Cunning Little Vixen*, and Prokofiev's *The Love for Three Oranges*.

---

* One of the best introductions to this history is Mahony, Latimer, and Folmsbee's invaluable *Illustrators of Children's Books: 1744–1945*, 3rd ed. (Boston: The Horn Book, 1970).
† See Forrest Reid's *Illustrators of the Eighteen Sixties*, originally published in 1928 and recently reprinted by Dover Books—as well as Gleeson White's *English Illustration: The Sixties*, first published in 1897 and reprinted by Kingsmead Reprints, Bath, England in 1970.

This volume, presenting examples (chosen by the editor) of Victorian color picture books, is introduced by a conversation with Maurice Sendak that took place at Mr. Sendak's country home. The works we talked about (and the English editions of the works reproduced in this volume) are listed as follows:

RANDOLPH CALDECOTT

Hey Diddle Diddle and *Baby Bunting* [First edition, 1882]

WALTER CRANE

1, 2, Buckle My Shoe [Sixpenny Picture Toy Book, first published in 1868, this edition *circa* 1871]

Selections from *Beauty and the Beast, The Frog Prince,* and *An Alphabet of Old Friends* [Shilling Picture Toy Books, first published in 1863, these editions *circa* 1871]

Selections from *The Baby's Bouquet* [First edition, 1879]

KATE GREENAWAY

Selections from *Mother Goose* [First published in 1881, this edition *circa* 1881–82]

E. V. B.

Selections from *A New Child's Play* [First published in 1877, this second edition published in 1879]

Selections from *The Story without an End* [First edition, 1868]

ANONYMOUS

Selections from *Puss-in-Boots, Jack and the Bean-stalk,* and *Tom Thumb* (in *Our Nurse's Picture Book*) [*Circa* early 1870s, probably 1871]

RICHARD DOYLE AND ANDREW LANG

The Princess Nobody [First Edition, 1884—with the omission of the final text illustration depicting the Prince and Princess sitting on a Rose. The illustrations of the Elves dancing at dusk (pp. 130–31) and sleeping in the tree (pp. 132–33), which appear to interrupt the story, as well as other discrepancies in the relation of illustrations to text, have been retained exactly as they appeared in the original.]

RICHARD DOYLE

Selections from *In Fairyland* ("Triumphal March of the Elf-King" and "The Fairy Queen Takes an Airy Drive") [Reproduced from the second edition published in 1875]

"ALEPH"

Geographical Fun [*Circa* late 1860s]

R. M. BALLANTYNE

The Butterfly's Ball [First published in 1857, this edition *circa* early 1860s]

Jonathan Cott

A Dialogue
with Maurice Sendak

During a question-and-answer session at the Library of Congress in 1970, you stated that "England invented the children's book as we know it." Were you referring to an early nineteenth-century book like The Butterfly's Ball *or to the highly elaborate wedding of text and pictures that one finds in the work of the great nineteenth-century illustrators?*

I was thinking of Randolph Caldecott, whose work, to me, heralds the beginning of the picture book.

You wouldn't then start off with the early Walter Crane toy and picture books?

Crane's things are beautiful. But there isn't that wedding you mentioned, that special marriage. I mean, with Crane there are gorgeous images: great big, full-color, ornamental, flamboyant images *sitting* in a book. Again, they are pictures that are inserted *into* a text; they're proper but old-fashioned. You get somebody like Caldecott—and there may be intermediary people—but I'm leaping to Caldecott because with him there is a juxtaposition of picture and word, there's a counterpoint which never happened before. Words are left out and the picture says it. Pictures are left out and the word says it. It's like a balancing ball, it goes back and forth. And this, to me, is the invention of the picture book.

Crane is always a better designer than Caldecott, and his books are exquisitely put together. But they don't have that kind of spontaneous, intuitive quality which I identify with a picture book for young people—almost a stream of consciousness, a rushing, impending movement. Crane didn't think of children's books like that, I don't think he had that particular kind of mind. And I think Caldecott did, without knowing it. And Beatrix Potter did. . . . So, when I talked about England inventing the children's picture book, I was thinking, not of *Goody Two-Shoes*, not of *The Butterfly's Ball*, not even of Crane, but of the Caldecott of *Hey Diddle Diddle* and *Baby Bunting*, where you laugh at the picture because the word isn't there and where you almost hear the music that's punctuated by an image rather than a word. It's wonderful.

I think it would be interesting if you'd talk about these two particular Caldecott works which were originally published together and which we are reproducing here.

Hey Diddle Diddle and *Baby Bunting* perfectly demonstrate what I meant when I talked about the beginnings of the modern picture book. For in these two works you find a rhythmic syncopation between words and images—a syncopation which is both delightful and highly musical.

On the jacket of the book you see the cat playing his fiddle to the puzzled baby, and it serves as an overture to what follows. With the first picture you have the cat introducing himself to the children, bowing down, violin in hand. And in the first color illustration, which also starts off in a musical way, the children are dancing at a party.

On the next two pages you see the cat and then two adults examining the fiddle. Caldecott often interjects people into an animal fantasy, as if he were, in a consciously funny way, reminding us that it is we, the readers, who are watching over the shoulders of the characters to observe what's going on—in this case, checking out the fiddle.

Now, the next two pages are perfect Caldecott. In most versions of this rhyme, the cow literally jumps over the moon. But here, the cow is merely jumping: the moon is on the horizon in the background and, in this perspective, only gives the *appearance* of being under the cow. In this way Caldecott is being exceedingly logical, since he obviously knows the cow can't jump over the moon. But within that logic he shows you, on the color page, two pigs dancing, the moon smiling, the hen and the rooster carrying on— all of it is perfectly acceptable to him and to us. But Caldecott won't go beyond a certain "logical" point: the cow *seems* to be jumping over the moon, yet in fact it's just leaping on the ground . . . and, still, this is bizarre enough to make the milkmaid drop her pail of milk.

Now there's a point to her dumping over the milk, for when you turn the page to read "The Little Dog laughed to see such fun," you might well have taken this line as a reference to the cow's having jumped over the moon, but in fact it's referring to the fact that the milk—or whatever was in that pail—is now being gobbled up by the two pigs, while the cow is staring from the corner, watching it all happen; the maid looking down, perplexed, perhaps annoyed. So Caldecott has interjected a whole new story solely by means of the illustrations, adding and ramifying like a theme-and-variations—just building, on top of the line, image upon image.

And from this absurdity and silliness, you turn the page to find one of his greatest and most beautiful pictures—"And the Dish ran away with the Spoon." Here, the dancing is continuing, with the same cat, back again, playing his violin, but this time for the pleasure of objects in the kitchen—a flask, dishes, bowls—and in the foreground you see the dish running away with the spoon. It's a very dramatic image. And you can almost hear the music coming from the back room as you observe the couple fleeing, obviously in love.

And when you turn again, the rhyme ends in catastrophe: the dish is broken, the spoon is being hustled away by her furious parents (the fork and the knife), and the other dishes, very unhappy, are looking at the dish lying in smithereens on the floor.

So it all ends in tragedy. The pounding, musical quality of the book culminates in this strange ending note. And that's Caldecott: words taking on unobvious meanings, colors, and dramatic qualities. He *reads* into things, and this, of course, is what the illustrator's job is really all about—to interpret the text much as a musical conductor interprets a score.

Now we move on to *Baby Bunting*—he's the little fat creature sitting on the chair. And as you turn the page to see him dancing, you're aware of Caldecott's continuing to carry over the physical—if not orchestral—movement of *Hey Diddle Diddle*. (I continually talk about the musical and contrapuntal quality of Caldecott's work because I literally hear music as I turn the pages!)

But this situation is a bit more conventional than the one depicted in *Hey Diddle Diddle:* the baby's getting dressed, father's going a-hunting, looking a little ridiculous as he disappears behind a wall, followed by that wonderful dog trotting after him whom we next see with its rear end poking out of the bushes or appearing at the side of the page, the father frantically hunting. But the hunting is ineffectual, and all comes to naught. So they rush off to town to buy a rabbit skin. And this, of course, is pure Caldecott: the father dressed in hunting regalia with his dog, unable to kill a rabbit, finally winding up in town to *buy* the skin.

So he brings it home to wrap the Baby Bunting in, and what follows is a scene of jollity: the baby dressed in that silly garment, everyone rushing around, pictures on the walls from other Caldecott picture books, then a lovely illustration of Mama and Baby.

And now again Caldecott does the unexpected. The rhyme ends ("To wrap the Baby Bunting in"), but as you turn the page you see Baby and mother strolling—Baby dressed in that idiotic costume with the ears poking out of his head—and up on the little hillside a group of about nine rabbits playing. And the Baby—I'd give anything to have the original drawing of that baby!—Baby is staring with the *most* perplexed look at those rabbits, as though with the dawning of knowledge that that lovely, cuddly, warm costume he's wrapped up in has *come* from those creatures. It's all in that baby's eye—just two lines, two mere dashes of the pen, but it's done so expertly that they absolutely express . . . well, anything you want to read into them. I read: astonishment, dismay at life— is this where rabbit skins come from? Does something have to die to dress me?

And after the lightness of the preceding scenes, we again hear that poignant note. Caldecott is too careful and too elegant an artist to become melodramatic; he never forces an issue, he just touches it lightly. And you can't say it's a tragedy, but something hurts. Like a shadow passing over very quickly. And it is this which gives a Caldecott book—however frothy its rhythms, verse, and pictures—an unexpected depth at any given point within the work, and its special value.

I'd like to get back to Walter Crane for a minute since we're reproducing several of his works: an early Sixpenny Toy Book (1, 2, Buckle My Shoe) and selections from several Shilling Picture Books and from The Baby's Bouquet. *Percy Muir, in his* Victorian Illustrated Books, *writes of Caldecott as a "true illustrator" and of Crane as a "decorator" who overindulges in tricky, mannerist effects. From what you said earlier, I take it that you would partially agree with Muir.*

I would just say that Crane was doing something very different from Caldecott. Crane is a decorator, but that's not a negative word. His decorations are beautiful, the embellishments are spellbinding, and the pages are exquisitely designed with an extra-ordinary attention to detail. Just look at his magnificent illustrations for *Beauty and the Beast,* for example.

In his lectures entitled Line and Form, *Crane divided art into two classes: one, the imitative, springing directly from nature; two, the imaginative, which he approved of and practiced. Do you think this distinction helps to explain Crane's formalistic approach?*

Yes, his work has the semblance of naturalism, but it's really pure fantasy/image-making. His colors, arrangements, patterns, and conceptions are purely imaginative. Which is what makes him so good. You can observe this even in the early *1, 2, Buckle My Shoe*. Obviously, he adored Japanese painting, and this is practically an homage to that art. Just look at the arrangements and at the figures on page 32:* the simple rendering, the flat black shape of the boy's clothes. It's very Oriental—that's where the influence came from. And I think what was wonderful was that he simply turned it into Walter Crane. He didn't, like so many people, just draw Japanese illustrations, or whatever. His flat patterning and simple formal shapes have a personal quality all their own.

But of course there's something terribly English about Crane. These women's faces are so obviously Victorian. If you observe most of the artists' work of that period, all the women are conventionally rendered; it's simply the typical look of the time. Even Tenniel didn't attempt a uniquely personalized portrait of Alice; he just gave her an English Alice face. And so in Crane, too, it's hard to see *through* the Victorian veneer. These are faces that are just *put on*. You can notice this in *Beauty and the Beast* . . . and here, too: they're almost glib faces. There's no attempt at portraiture or at conveying character. And this *is* a lack, but then again, Crane is a designer. And you can't blame him for not doing what he didn't want to do; it wasn't his *forte*.

Now, in a sense, you can also blame Caldecott for this same look. His women and men all have those clean-cut, good-looking, Victorian-lined faces. But they're livelier. They're infinitely more personable. And his milkmaids—maybe their faces don't convey very much, but their bodies and attitudes certainly do. He shows more through the body than Crane ever did. Crane was too formal and rigid, but, as I said before, he didn't *want* to show any more than he did.

Now, coming to *The Baby's Bouquet*: what makes this book—and its companion volumes *The Baby's Opera* and *The Baby's Own Aesop*—so imaginative is simply the incredible amount of *variation* on every page—the wonderful variation of shapes, sizes, and colors. And because of that I don't for one minute miss the lack of psychological depth; I think it's ridiculous to demand that everything should have it.

Look at pages 52–53 ("The Old Man in Leather"): the colors are beautiful, the printing is gorgeous (thanks to Edmund Evans), the variations of sizes, of figures, of colors, of shapes—repeating the moon shape on this page, the moon shape on the other . . . it's exquisite! Or look at the black cats on the *ABC* page (p. 60): one, two, three, four black cats, with little black socks . . . and the little black textures carried over there and the little blacks down here. Perhaps no one looking at this page is going to examine it in this particular way, but your eye is going to take it in and you're going to be extremely pleased. So too with the circles on the four corners of page 57 ("The North Wind & The Robin") and then the circle of the woman's cape on the opposite page. Crane carries shapes through the entire book—whether he did it consciously or not makes no difference—he did it because he was a great, instinctive designer.

And this is a terribly difficult book to illustrate because every page has music on it. Just leafing through, you find "If All The World Were Paper" (p. 61). The colors and the relationships are dazzling: all the little shapes and the smoke from the pipe and then the little leaves here . . . all the arabesques. They're not arbitrary, they're as tight

---

* In all cases, Mr. Sendak's page references designate the page numbers in this volume. [Ed.]

as they could be. And look at those squares. It's almost an abstraction. It *is* an abstraction!

Then pages 62–63 ("The Little Disaster")—it's wonderful. Here Crane has a whole story—almost like a sequence of animated drawings. Look at these two birds that form this entire pattern up in the sky. He misses nothing . . . the little fruits falling from the tree. And notice how the sun has changed position: one, it's just rising; two, it's in the sky; and then it's going up into the sky and out of the picture.

And here's "Looby Light" and "Margery Daw" (pp. 55, 64): all the figures dancing, people being crushed by borders, spiders dangling from edges. I mean, kids see this, you must know, kids see everything. Most adults don't, perhaps, but children poring over a book will see every one of these things.

As for his contents page (p. 50), Crane is one of the great contents-page-people. And title-page-people and book-jacket-people and cover-people . . . he's a superb designer. Just looking through this book makes me admire Crane tremendously. One can enjoy him a lot more in a work like this than in his formal picture books where there's less opportunity for him to do anything but pictures. When Crane does something like the line drawings for the Edgeworth books, he's less interesting to me. Without color Crane seems less appealing, you get a feeling that he's just producing inserted illustrations, and he doesn't give himself the opportunity to do as much as he can. But *The Baby's Bouquet* is marvelous.

I gather you're not a great admirer of Kate Greenaway's work, but I'd like to ask you about her illustrations for Mother Goose *that we're reproducing here.*

I like this almost best of any Kate Greenaway, perhaps because it's in the tradition of Crane. I mean, how can you *not* like a title page like this one?

When people criticize Greenaway, it's usually because of what they consider to be her arcadian preciosity—her dimity-clad maidens and demure little boys.

What I don't like about Greenaway is her inability to draw. And the fact that she went on and on and never really improved: there is a vapidness in much of her work. But in this book she's contained all these images in little borders, and that's when she was at her best. In her *Almanacs* she was very good, too, for when she gave herself a "small" place to work, she'd fill it beautifully. But when she was illustrating a picture book—*Pied Piper*, for example—the worst of her graphic problems became apparent.

As for her idea of "Mother Goose," it's a bust. I mean, she didn't know Mother Goose from a hole in the wall. She imposed herself on everything she did and turned it into Kate Greenaway, in the same way that Arthur Rackham did. And she really was oblivious to how much you could do with a book. She makes precise little images, and they are beautiful, but they stop at that. The pretty picture for each verse: that's not going to involve any child. It's easy, it's lovely to look at, it doesn't tax the brain or the heart. And that's what I think, generally, most people prefer. But in my terms, it isn't sufficient to illustrate a Mother Goose book in this way.

But isn't there another way to look at Greenaway's work—to see in her "sublimated" images a slightly neurasthenic tension resulting, in part, from her having attempted to convey a sense of incorruptibility?

That, so far as I'm concerned, is looking at something that simply isn't there. I'd hate to apply that kind of explanation all the time because it gets a little dull. I once wrote a review of various Mother Goose books and criticized this one for particular reasons. And just looking at this verse—"Goosey, goosey, gander,/Where shall I wander" (it's a very funny verse, it's practically a haiku, and, like most other Mother Goose verses, you don't know exactly what it means)—reminds me how much I disliked this particular Greenaway illustration (p. 71). She has two little girls rushing up to bed, one of whom has a look almost of distaste, as if to say: "There you are, Goosey, don't come near me." And that's generally the look of a Greenaway book—"Stay away from my door, you evil-type things, wherever you may be." It's a "pure" world, it's a "clean" world. Everybody's dress is spotless.

Anyway, I used to be harsher on things like this and say: What do we need a book like this for? Now my feeling is: Why not? It's a perfectly attractive book. She has Little Bo Peep here (p. 70), and it's an atrocious drawing of a little girl. It's all there, but it's boring. What makes it bearable is that it's pretty. If it were an awful-looking book, I'd hate it. But it has her printer Edmund Evans going for it, it has her acute sense of design and its own peculiar honesty: she does create her own world. And if it isn't Mother Goose in my terms, it's Mother Goose in hers.

I'm sure you wouldn't feel the same way about Beatrix Potter.

No, not at all. Beatrix Potter is a genius. Greenaway is a decorator, and, to me, not as good as Crane. Beatrix Potter was also a real writer, and she would never have done a book that was so obviously meant to please adults the way Greenaway did. I think Greenaway has proved a much worse influence on twentieth-century children's books than any other of that whole group. There's a proliferation of terrible books similar to this, but they're nowhere as good as Greenaway, nowhere as good.

But what about the shadings and textures of Greenaway's work at her best?

Yes, they're ravishing. Where she succeeds, as on "Lucy Locket" and especially "Cross Patch" (p. 68), she's wonderful. She conveys more through shape and color than through any interpretive powers, of which, in my opinion, she had none. But she does have aesthetic powers, and she gets away with a lot because of her marvelous sense of color and exquisite taste. A hair-split away and she was done for. A hair-split away was the twentieth century, during which books like this were produced ad nauseam, and continue to be—books which don't have her taste, her sense of color, her sense of patterning and designing.

Kate Greenaway once wrote: "You can go into a beautiful new country if you stand under a large apple tree and look up to the blue sky through the white flowers. I suppose I went to it very young before I could really remember and that is why I have such a wild delight in cowslips and apple-blossom—they always give me the strange feeling of trying to remember, *as if I had known them in a former world." Don't you think that what Greenaway was at least attempting to convey in her work was this sense of remembered childhood?*

She remembers what she'd like to remember, of course, but her memory is severely censored. I really don't think that she got anywhere close to real childhood. And, to expand on what I said before, I don't think a book like *Mother Goose* is really a children's book. It's what an adult would go into a store and buy, thinking: "This is perfect for little Jane." But what he or she is truly saying is: "It's perfect for me. It frightens me not; it daunts me not. It's pretty, it's lovable—I can even put it under my pillow and not have a nightmare. Thus, it must be good for my child."

Children may have loved Greenaway, they probably still do. But this really is a book for safe adulthood, with the preconception and warped view of a saccharined childhood that most of the human race never has experienced. We have moments of it, but that isn't what childhood is all about. People don't rush around in the golden sunshine looking like this, they just simply don't. And most Victorian children certainly didn't.

So this depiction is almost counter-phobic and contrary to what was existing during that period. But that's not bad. At one time, I would have condemned Greenaway for ignorance, for closing her eyes to the realities of life. *Let* her close her eyes if she can conceive of something as pretty as this—the dream of apple blossoms *is* real, though screened. But, then again, who really has done that much more? Arthur Hughes was illustrating around that time, too, and he occasionally drew as badly as Greenaway and didn't have any of Crane's sense of design and didn't know about color—his illustrations are always in black and white—yet his pictures convey a kind of fearful reverberation of genuine childhood. That's what illustration really is all about, but in any generation there aren't very many artists like Arthur Hughes. . . . Kate Greenaway? She made very pretty books and satisfied lots of people.

We're including selections from A New Child's Play *and* The Story without an End *by Eleanor Vere Boyle (a.k.a. E. V. B.). Throughout her career as an illustrator, the depiction in her work of states of madness became more and more extreme—and, in fact, she herself went mad at the end of her life. What strikes me as most significant about her illustrations is the way she, unlike someone like Kate Greenaway, continually revealed an obsessive sense of sexual confusion (little boys seen as little girls)—and this, along with her death-haunted, disembodied style, makes her seem both perverse and fascinating today. Do you agree?*

Not at all. I think there's something absolutely revolting about E. V. B.'s work. She's doing something which is perverse—I don't know what to call it—but I recoil from it. And it's not just the thing that you mentioned—the sexual confusion concerning girls and boys. Not only does she draw badly, which offends me right off as an artist, but her conceptions are gross and vulgar, and she doesn't have those fine things going for her that Greenaway and Crane did. She's not a good designer. Her lettering is bad, her drawing is bad, and there's that "perverse" view of hers which just turns me off. I mean, a picture like "Trip and goe, heave and hoe" (p. 79) —it's not that they're *either* boys or girls, they might even be women and men, they might even be pregnant or not, they could be anything. . . . I just can't talk about her from a rational perspective.

Let me try to explain my interest in E. V. B. by quoting from Susan Sontag's discussion concerning the revival of interest in the French "primitive" photographer Atget. She writes: "The judgment of Atget as 'not a fine technician' that Weston made in his Day-books *perfectly reflects the coherence of Weston's view and his distance from contemporary taste. . . . Weston notes: '[Atget's] instinct for subject matter was keen, but his recording weak—his construction inexcusable.' . . . It is precisely imperfect technique that breaks the bland equation of 'nature' and 'beauty.' . . . Darker, history-laden models of beauty have inspired a revaluation of the photography of the past and, in an apparent revulsion against beauty, recent generations of photographers stand ready to show the pain, the disorder of the world. But notwithstanding the aims of indiscreet, unposed, informal, often harsh photography—to reveal 'truth,' not beauty—photography still beautifies. At the very least, the real has a pathos. And that pathos is—beauty."*

I don't believe that E. V. B. is an example of someone you could talk about in this context. I think her work just reveals a collapse of technique, of taste, and of art. This is blind work, and I think it would be mistaken to read something contemporary into it. Because E. V. B.'s work, to me, is a gross and terribly sentimental parody of childhood. I don't think it's ugly or meaningfully homely in the true sense. It's just a grotesque and shoddy book, and one for which I don't happen to have pity. And yes, I am very hostile to it because it represents a collapse of every standard of bookmaking. And it makes no sense, in my opinion, to see in this something of what Susan Sontag is writing about: to say, for instance, that in contrast to the pseudo-phoniness of a Kate Greenaway, E. V. B. gives a kind of "real" view. In a way, it might reflect the Victorian confusion of the sexes—who was what and why. You might bend it to fit such a theory, but to do so would be terribly sentimental.

I'm glad you're playing devil's advocate here, since I'm being very harsh. But you could take very bad drawings by people in mental institutions and make a case that they reflected our time and build up a whole cockamamie theory about them. I'm not denying the theory, I'm not denying that there could be work that would reflect just the thing that you're interested in. I'm just saying that it's fake to use *this* book or *this* artist's work as a sounding-board for that kind of theory. Because this illustration of "Hush-A-Bye, Baby" (p. 81) isn't an image of chaos or of the dissolution and disorder of the world; it's just a horrible drawing. E. V. B. was trying to do something interesting, but she was incapable of doing it, and so she wound up with just a rather bizarre image. But the bizarre image comes about through faulty art.

Now, you can look at something like the work of Fuseli, who *does* create bizarre images, but he knew what he was doing. E. V. B. has tried to draw a baby falling out of a cradle, but what you see is finally nothing but a 90-year-old bald man falling out of a tree. It's an atrocity. And to say that she was doing something mystical or deep is to give her much too much credit.

We're also including selections from some early 1870s picture books—strong, outsized, full-page illustrations for stories like Puss-in-Boots *and* Jack *and the Bean-stalk. (Some of these illustrations are even thought to be based on designs by Kate Greenaway.)*

They're almost hallucinatory, very much like the illustrations by Thomas Nast in his McLaughlin books, which are *really* hallucinations. Now, one of the effects here is purely physical, in that they give you the sense of being *inside* the book. And for a small person looking at this, it must be even more overwhelming—you can really climb into the page. The drawings in *Jack and the Bean-stalk* are very operatic, they're like stage productions. And they give you a sense of photographic close-up effects as well. . . . Some of these *Puss-in-Boots* illustrations, of course, are almost campy in our terms. But they're so clever. They're done not only with technical skill but with wit.

I'm never interested in these books specifically as children's books. That's dull. What makes them interesting is the fact that they're both for children and for everybody else. In my opinion there's no such thing as a book *just* for children.

In 1870, Richard Doyle's magnificent In Fairyland *appeared with a poetry text by William Allingham. Andrew Lang liked the Doyle illustrations so much that he wrote a prose text for the same pictures, and the result of this collaboration was a book entitled* The Princess Nobody—*a work which is beautiful in its own right and which we're reproducing here (followed by two stunning illustrations from the original work not included in the Doyle-Lang collaboration).*

Well, what are you going to say about Doyle? He's probably the best of them all. He's sensational. He has all the accoutrements of the Victorian illustrator—the girls look right, for example—but he's one of the better draftsmen, he has the cleverest mind, the most gorgeous sense of color, and a fantastic imagination. And these are obviously some of his very best drawings. But almost everything he did—especially the illustrations for *The King of the Golden River* and Mark Lemon's *The Enchanted Doll*—is extraordinary.

And why are these things so beautiful? Because immediately, when you look at them, you know he's doing something more than illustrating; there's some insidious purpose behind it all. Look at those sleeping elves (pp. 132–133) or at the frontispiece! You can't and shouldn't analyze it. Actually, this particular frontispiece illustration is like a parody of Blake with those writhing female figures and little boy angels falling out of flowers. There's a lot of what could be considered tacky sentiment here . . . with those girls doing a ballet around the pistils. And then there's this little monster at the bottom—right out of a Wagner opera—tormenting a butterfly. Yet Doyle manages to cut sentiment nicely, something very few Victorian illustrators could do. But again, there's not much you can say about Doyle. We're in complete agreement here: he is just one of the super artists, and you don't have to know what it is he's doing. It doesn't have to be spelled out, it really doesn't. The fact that it works and that it conveys itself instantly to you—that's what illustration is all about.

We're reproducing a book entitled Geographical Fun, *consisting of a series of twelve maps of European countries drawn by a fifteen-year-old girl who went under the name of* "Aleph"; *it's a charming little work and really doesn't require comment. Like all the other works we've talked about, this book is an example of Victorian color lithography. But recently I came across a fascinating picture book consisting of eight colored wood-blocks by R. M. Ballantyne—best known as the author of "boy's books" like* Coral Island, Ungara, *and* The Dog Crusoe. *Ballantyne's illustrations for an adaptation of William Roscoe's* The Butterfly's Ball—*originally published in 1807 and one of the first and most fanciful poems written for children—have a quality that suggests—perhaps only slightly—the almost "psychical" shapes and curves in the paintings of someone like Arshile Gorky.*

On hindsight, we can see in the accidental effects of the woodcut process a kind of pre-monition and foreshadowing of expressionist art, but this isn't really the important point. All the care that went into the printing of the works of Crane, Caldecott, and Green-away—all those details and delicacies that Edmund Evans was concerned with—are dumped overboard in a book like this; it turns the argument upside down.

The drawings are rough-hewn—very direct, robust, and unpretentious. But in their crudity they have a conviction and liveliness that I personally never find in the work of someone like Greenaway. They're abstracted into patterns and designs that give a tre-mendous vitality to the page. And this makes the poem come to life. It's so flagrantly different from the books we've been looking at.

And, in a strange way, there is something intangible about these illustrations that sug-gests, in their roughness of expression, a kind of Blakean feeling that's extremely affecting. They're not well drawn or well conceived, but they catch something that a more cun-ningly devised and self-conscious approach would have missed altogether. And after all that Victoriana, it comes as a tremendous relief to the eye. The fancy elegance of the poem is beautifully offset by the almost blatant quality of the pictures. And that counter-point makes it an exciting and modern book: the illustrations aren't just pasted along-side the words, imitating them like a tedious echo. Rather, by expressing the words, they reveal another sound and, at the same time, tighten up the poem and give a life to the creatures that they don't really have in the poem itself.

More generally, I wanted to ask you about the following statement by Lewis Carroll: "My ambition now is to be read by children from nought to five. To be read? Nay, not so! Say rather to be thumbed, to be cooed-over, to be dog's-eared, to be rumpled, to be kissed by the illiterate, ungrammatical, dimpled darlings." Do you think that a child's first response to a book is that of tactile enjoyment?

Certainly I think it would be *part* of a child's reaction. But as to what Carroll says, there's something quite nauseating about that quotation.

It sounds to me as if Carroll thinks of himself as the book that's going to be receiving all that affection!

I agree wholeheartedly. But it also reflects a kind of sentimental, pursed-mouth view of Victorian childhood. A more vigorous re-saying of this, however, should certainly affirm that children do experience this very sensuous pleasure in objects: a book *is* more than just something to read . . . it's something that you want to touch. And when you're designing and binding books, this awareness certainly affects your work: that just the touch and smell and *hold* of a book is as much part of the pleasure in reading it as is anything else. Especially with kids, who don't lose the pleasure of sensuous experiences, who enjoy touching and feeling and smelling.

You yourself once said: "In the way a dream comes to us at night, feelings come to me, and then I must rush to put them down. But these fantasies have to be given physical form, so you build a house around them, and the house is what you call a story, and the painting of the house is the bookmaking. But essentially it's a dream, or it's a fantasy." I found this a beautiful idea—that of a book being a clothed or embodied manifestation.

That's really what form is. Because the impulse to create, the idea for a book, *is* a feeling—a vivid emotion—and the artist's job is to give it some palpable shape so that it means something to somebody else. It isn't a work of art just because it arises from a genuine creative emotion; everybody has that. And that's why I object to people saying: "Children are wonderful artists, everything they do is gorgeous." It's true, but they can't take the next step, which is to give it form. And why should they? They're children, and experience and age are necessary. You get the idea, there's this wonderful palpitating thing, and then you construct a form—words, pictures, the shape of the book, the binding, the cover. Everything.

What about the forms of the books we've looked at today?

They're beautiful. I mean, look at the form of Greenaway's *Mother Goose.* It's beautiful because it's so accurate. It's small, it's easy to handle, it's precious—but in the best sense of that word. She's kept everything miniaturized and jewel-like—very personal and intimate. And it's like opening a casket and finding a necklace or diamond earring in it; there's that quality of intimacy.

The Caldecott books are very sloppily done; in fact, they come apart. And yet that's right for Caldecott: there's a kind of breeziness and unaffectedness about his work that makes you want to flip through his books and watch those drawings *zing* and *animate* before your eyes, like a child's flip book. His form is right, and even the way the book was bound is right. . . . Then you look at Crane, with his ornate and statuesque bindings and his *zaftig* shapes and book sizes. And that's right, too. He's a designer first and foremost. . . . Doyle's forms are almost always small, aren't they? Because there's a kind of mischievous *quickness* to his drawings that you wouldn't want to see on big, exploded pages . . . except for *In Fairyland* where you have grandiose paintings, and they're quite beautiful. But, as I said before, I prefer *The King of the Golden River* and the Mark Lemon books in which Doyle is working small. Because with his pen he's best, in my opinion; he kind of squirts across a page without taking up much room. And the sharpness and quickness of the size is one of his most attractive qualities. . . . So each of these artists has his particular way of working, according to what his own vision of the work is. And the forms are appropriate and beautiful.

This section of Victorian illustration is, of course, devoted specifically to color books . . .

And I think you're right to emphasize this aspect. After all, this is a period during which the development of color was brought to such a point of finesse that you really wouldn't want to miss seeing examples of it.

We know what Victorian England was like with its layers of social injustice. But it's also true that this was a time when there was a pleasure in expanding and experimenting with printing, and when you also had a true sense of craftsmanship and apprenticeship. Today, our equipment is better, we know more than Evans did, and we can do more. But there seems to be a lack of the sense of craftsmanship. Consequently, most books today look very *ersatz*—not put together with love, but *manufactured*. It's very costly to achieve what I'm talking about, and when, finally, you do achieve it, you wonder if it's worth it, because the expense is so inordinate that no one can afford the result.

But coming back to our opening discussion about the picture book phenomenon starting in England: I always think of that period—the earlier-to-middle part of the nineteenth century and then onward—as being like a flamboyant burst of energy. It seems that socially, historically, and geographically everything was right for it to happen in England. The art, talent, and experience were there, and it all came together and exploded. Starting with William Blake and going on to Samuel Palmer and Calvert; from the romantic painters to the illustrators, there was a constant, supercharged, energetic force working in England. And then it emerged in picture books during the great period of the 1860s and '70s.

Whose work represents the "end" to you?

Arthur Rackham, to me, is a dead end. If you compare *The Wind in the Willows* illustrations done by Rackham and E. H. Shepard, you can see that Shepard is the real illustrator, who bites into characters, and Rackham the big, inert superstar—the monster craftsman, a really glorious painter, but he doesn't have the beginnings of the illustrator's instinct.

It's strange, but I think mainly of Americans who worked in and enlarged this tradition: Howard Pyle, N. C. Wyeth, E. W. Kemble, A. B. Frost, Nast, and even Winslow Homer, who was never much thought of as an illustrator but who was a magnificent one.

Finally, I wanted to ask you to say something more about your refusal to make a distinction between a book for children and a book for adults.

Yes, I don't draw that distinction except in the obvious sense that a child isn't going to read Ernest Hemingway. The fact is that in past times most children weren't expected to live past a certain age. There really wasn't time for childhood. And then you had the situation in which children were supposed to read hair-raising, admonitory accounts of how one should look at one's little brother lying in a coffin and not get upset.

Now that was extreme. But we, too, have a bizarre concept of childhood. We prolong childhood ad nauseam. I mean, the fact that Peter Pan is so popular gives you a quick, disturbing idea of our concept of childhood. But the older idea was just as bad in its own way—for then there was no point at which a child could be a child.

Now with Caldecott, we find what is basically a children's book. The wonder of it, however, is that anyone can read and be moved by it. But really, it's something done for children, and it's like saying: "We know that childhood now exists, there's time to sit back and be a kid for a while and enjoy it."

Randolph Caldecott

Hey Diddle Diddle
AND
Baby Bunting

Hey Diddle Diddle

HEY DIDDLE DIDDLE.

Hey, diddle, diddle,

The Cat

and the Fiddle,

The Cow jumped over the Moon,

The little Dog laughed

to see such fun,

And the Dish ran away with the Spoon.

Baby Bunting

BABY BUNTING.

Bye, Baby Bunting!

Father's

gone

a-hunting,

Gone to fetch

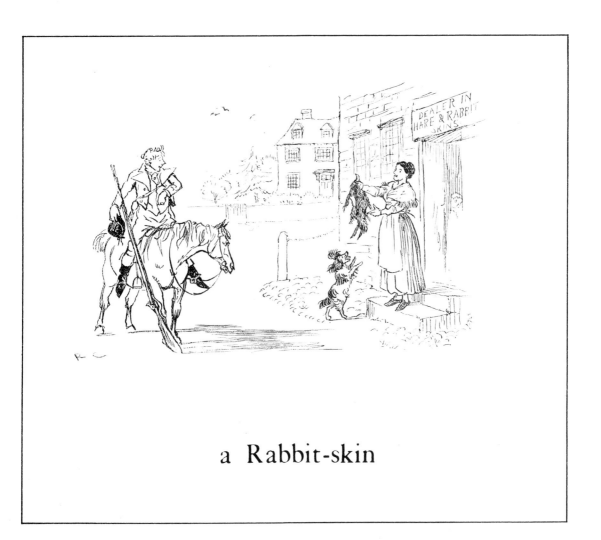

a Rabbit-skin

To wrap the Baby Bunting in.

Walter Crane

1, 2, Buckle My Shoe

Beauty and the Beast
(SELECTIONS)

The Frog Prince
(SELECTIONS)

An Alphabet of Old Friends
(SELECTIONS)

The Baby's Bouquet
(SELECTIONS)

1, 2. One Two,
Buckle my shoe.
3, 4. Three, Four,
Open the door.

5, 6. Five, Six, Pick up sticks. 7, 8. Seven, Eight, Lay them straight.

11, 12. Eleven, Twelve,
Ring the Bell.

15, 16. Fifteen, Sixteen,
Maids in the Kitchen.

19, 20. Nineteen, Twenty.
My plate is empty.

Beauty and the Beast

The Frog Prince

An Alphabet of Old Friends

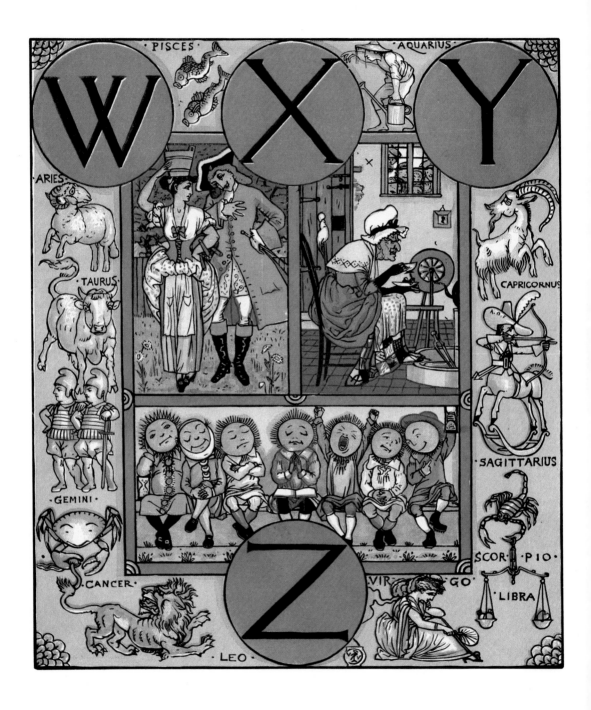

The Baby's Bouquet

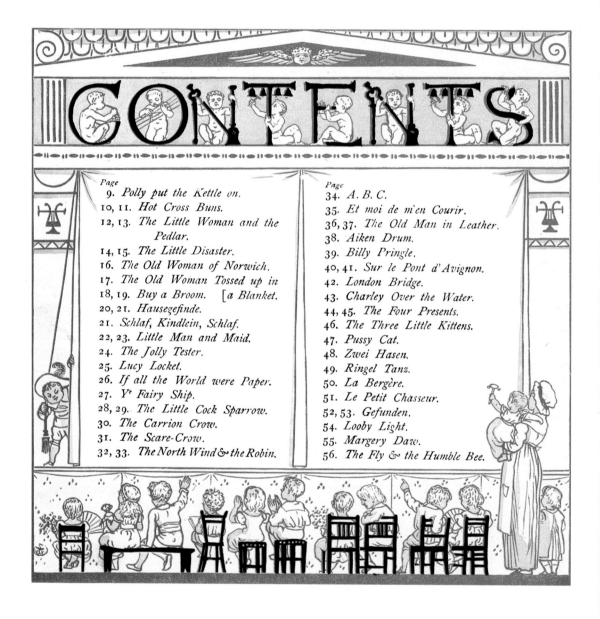

CONTENTS

2 En passant auprès d'un étang
  Où les canards chantaient,
  Où les canards chantaient
Dans leur joli chant ils disaient ;
" Cancan, cancan, cancan, cancan,"
Et moi qui croyais qu'ils disaient.
" Jett' le dedans, jett' le dedans,"
Et moi de m'en cour', cour', cour',
  Et moi de m'en courir !

3 En passant devant une maison,
  Où la bonn' femm' chantait,
  Où la bonn' femm' chantait ;
Dans son joli chant ell' disait
" Dodo, dodo, dodo, dodo,"
Et moi qui croyais qu'elle disait
" Cass' lui les os, cass' lui les os,"
Et moi de m'en cour', cour', cour',
  Et moi de m'en courir !

THE·LiTTLE·CoCK·SPaRRoW

A lit-tle cock-sparrow sat on a high tree, A lit-tle cock-sparrow sat
on a high tree, A lit-tle cock-spar-row sat on a high tree, And he
chirrupped, he chirrupped so mer-ri-ly. He chirrupped, he chirrupped, he
chirrupped, he chirrupped, He chirrupped, he chirrupped, he chirrupped, he chirrupped, A
lit-tle cock-sparrow sat on a high tree, And he chirrupped, he chirrupped so mer-ri-ly.

2 A naughty little boy with a bow and arrow,
Determined to shoot this little cock-sparrow ;

3 For this little cock-sparrow would make a nice stew,
And his giblets would make a nice little pie too.

4 "Oh, no," says cock-sparrow, "I won't make a stew,"
And he fluttered his wings, and away he flew.

If all the world were paper, And all the sea were ink,...... And all the trees were bread and cheese, What should we do for drink?

2 If all the world were sand—O!
Oh, then what should we lack—O!
If, as they say, there were no clay,
How should we take tobacco?

3 If all our vessels ran—a,
If none but had a crack,
If Spanish apes ate all the grapes,
How should we do for sack?

THE LITTLE DISASTER

2 And his dog he called Fidelle,
For he loved his master well;
And he had a little pony for his pleasure O!
In a sty not very big
He'd a frisky little pig,
Which he often called his little piggy treasure O!

3 Once his little maiden, Ann,
With her pretty little can,
Went a-milking when the morning sun was beaming O!
When she fell, I don't know how,
But she stumbled o'er the plough,
And the cow was quite astonished at her screaming O!

4 Little maid cried out in vain,
While the milk ran o'er the plain,
Little pig ran grunting after it so gaily O!
While the little dog behind,
For a share was much inclined,
So he pulled back squeaking piggy by the taily O!

5 Such a clatter now began
As alarmed the little man,
Who came capering from out his little stable O!
Pony trod on doggy's toes,
Doggy snapped at piggy's nose,
Piggy made as great a noise as he was able O!

6 Then to make the story short,
Little pony with a snort
Lifted up his little heels so very clever O!
And the man he tumbled down,
And he nearly cracked his crown,
And this only made the matter worse than ever O!

Kate Greenaway

Mother Goose

(SELECTIONS)

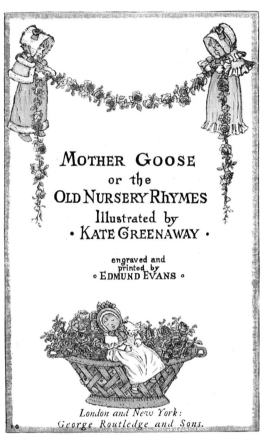

Lucy Locket, lost her pocket,
Kitty Fisher found it;
There was not a penny in it,
But a ribbon round it.

Cross Patch, lift the latch,
Sit by the fire and spin;
Take a cup, and drink it up,
Then call your neighbours in.

We`re all jolly boys, and we`re coming
with a noise,
Our stockings shall be made
Of the finest silk,
And our tails shall touch the ground.

Elsie Marley has grown so fine,
She won`t get up to serve the swine;
But lies in bed till eight or nine,
And surely she does take her time.

Draw a pail of water,
For my lady's daughter;
My father's a king, and my mother's a queen,
My two little sisters are dressed in green,
Stamping grass and parsley,
Marigold leaves and daisies.
One rush! two rush!
Pray thee, fine lady, come under my bush.

Little Bo-peep has lost her sheep,
And can't tell where to find them;
Leave them alone, and they'll come home,
And bring their tails behind them.

Goosey, goosey, gander,
Where shall I wander?
Up stairs, down stairs,
And in my lady's chamber:
There I met an old man,
Would not say his prayers;
Take him by the left leg,
Throw him down the stairs.

KG

A diller, a dollar,
A ten o'clock scholar;
What makes you come so soon?
You used to come at ten o'clock,
But now you come at noon!

KG

71

Little Betty Blue,
Lost her holiday shoe.
What will poor Betty do?
Why, give her another,
To match the other,
And then she will walk in two.

Mary, Mary, quite contrary,
How does your garden grow?
With silver bells, and cockle shells,
And cowslips all of a row.

See-Saw-Jack in the hedge,
Which is the way to London-bridge?

Humpty Dumpty sat on a wall,
Humpty Dumpty had a great fall.

One foot up, the other foot down,
That's the way to London-town.

Georgie Peorgie, pudding and pie,
Kissed the girls and made them cry;
When the girls begin to play,
Georgie Peorgie runs away.

All around the green gravel,
The grass grows so green,
And all the pretty maids are fit to be seen;
Wash them in milk,
Dress them in silk,
And the first to go down shall be married.

Ring-a-ring-a-roses,
A pocket full of posies;
Hush! hush! hush! hush!
We're all tumbled down.

E. V. B.
(Eleanor Vere Boyle)

A New Child's Play
(SELECTIONS)

AND

The Story without an End
(SELECTIONS)

Trip and goe, heave and hoe,
Up and down, to and fro,
From the town, to the grove
So merrily trip and goe

The little Boy in the Barn,
Lay down on some hay.
The Owl came out,
and flew about,
And the little Boy ran away.

Hush a bye baby on the tree top. —
When the wind blows, the cradle will rock:
When the bough breaks, —
The cradle will fall,
And down will come baby, and cradle, and all !

The Story without an End

LEIGHTON, BROS.

𝔏𝔬𝔫𝔤 𝔡𝔦𝔡 𝔥𝔦𝔰 𝔱𝔥𝔬𝔲𝔤𝔥𝔱𝔰 𝔴𝔞𝔟𝔢𝔯.

LEIGHTON, BROS.

The lark awakened visions of endless hopes.

LEIGHTON, BROS.

Earth Stars.

LEIGHTON, BROS.

When the Spring begins.

LEIGHTON, BROS.

A golden boat on a great, great water.

LEIGHTON, BROS.

The Lily, the flower of Heaven.

Anonymous

Puss-in-Boots
(SELECTIONS)

Jack and the Bean-stalk
(SELECTIONS)

Tom Thumb
(SELECTIONS)

Puss-in-Boots

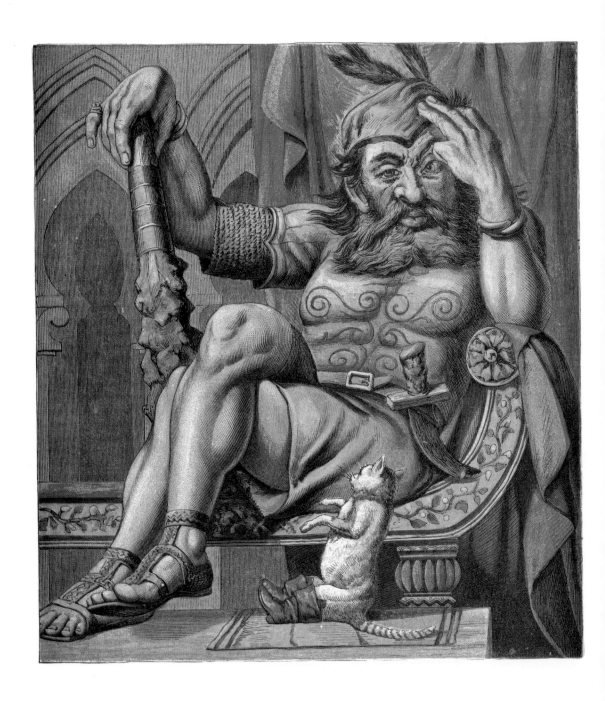

Jack and the Bean-stalk

Tom Thumb

Richard Doyle
AND
Andrew Lang

The Princess Nobody
AND
In Fairyland
(SELECTIONS)

THE PRINCESS NOBODY.

THE

PRINCESS NOBODY

A

TALE OF FAIRY LAND

BY

ANDREW LANG

AFTER THE DRAWINGS BY RICHARD DOYLE

PRINTED IN COLOURS BY EDMUND EVANS

LONDON

LONGMANS, GREEN, AND CO.

An Evening Ride.

BALLADE OF DEDICATION.

O all you babes at Branxholm Park,
This book I dedicate ;
A book for winter evenings dark,
Too dark to ride or skate.
I made it up out of my pate,
And wasted midnight oil,
Interpreting each cut and plate—
The works of DICKY DOYLE!

When weary winter comes, and hark!
The Teviot roars in "spate" ;
When half you think you'll need the Ark,
The flood's so fierce and great ;
Think of the Prince and of his mate,
Their triumph and their toil,
And mark them drawn in all their state—
The works of DICKY DOYLE!

Now, if my nonsense hits the mark—
If Wynnie, Pop, and Kate,
Think tales of Fays and Giants stark,
Not wholly out of date—
Another time, perchance, I'll prate,
And keep a merry coil,
Though ne'er I'll match the drawings great—
The works of DICKY DOYLE!

ENVOY.

Girls, may you ne'er know fear nor hate ;
Boys, field like Mr. Royle!
And, please, don't say I desecrate
The works of DICKY DOYLE!

Teasing a Butterfly.

THE PRINCESS NOBODY.
CHAPTER I.
THE PRINCESS NOBODY.

ONCE upon a time, when Fairies were much more common than they are now, there lived a King and a Queen. Their country was close to Fairy Land, and very often the little Elves would cross over the border, and come into the King's fields and gardens. The girl-fairies would swing out of the bells of the fuschias, and loll on the leaves, and drink the little drops of dew that fell down the stems. Here you may see all the Fairies making themselves merry at a picnic on a fuschia, and an ugly little Dwarf is climbing up the stalk.

10 *THE PRINCESS NOBODY.*

Here's the King, in mournful mood,
They'd amuse him, if they could!

Now the King and Queen of the country next to Fairy Land were
very rich, and very fond of each other; but one thing made them unhappy. They had no child, neither boy nor girl, to sit on the Throne
when they were dead and gone. Often the Queen said she wished she
had a child even if it were no bigger than her thumb; and she hoped
the Fairies might hear her and help her. But they never took any
notice. One day, when the King had been counting out his money all
day (the day when the tributes were paid in), he grew very tired. He
took off his crown and went into his garden. Then he looked all
round his kingdom and said, "Ah! I would give it all for a BABY!"

THE PRINCESS NOBODY. 11

No sooner had the King said this, than he heard a little squeaking voice near his foot: "You shall have a lovely Baby, if you will give me what I ask."

The King looked down, and there was the funniest little Dwarf that ever was seen. He had a high red cap like a flower. He had a big moustache, and a short beard that curled outwards. His cloak was red, like his cap, and his coat was green, and he rode on a green Frog. Many people would have been frightened, but the King was used to Fairies.

"You shall have a beautiful Baby, if you give me what I ask," said the Dwarf again.

"I'll give you anything you like," said the King.

"Then promise to give me NIENTE," said the Dwarf.

"Certainly," said the King (who had not an idea what NIENTE meant). "How will you take it?"

"I will take *it*," said the Dwarf, "in my own way, on my own day."

But the children were as jolly as ever, except one naughty baby,
and even *he* was petted, as you see!

111

12   *THE PRINCESS NOBODY.*

Here you see a Fairy host,
Fit to fight with Dwarf or Ghost.

With that he set spurs to his Frog, which cleared the garden path at one bound, and he was soon lost among the flowers.

Well, next day, a dreadful war broke out between the Ghosts and the Giants, and the King had to set forth and fight on the side of his friends the Giants.

A long, long time he was away; nearly a year. At last he came back to his own country, and he heard all the church bells ringing madly. "What *can* be the matter?" said the King, and hurried to his Palace, where all the Courtiers rushed out and told him the Queen had got a BABY.

"Girl or a boy?" says the King.

"A Princess, your Majesty," says the Nurse, with a low curtsey, correcting him.

Well, you may fancy how glad the King was, though he would have *preferred* a boy.

Here are little Birds in plenty,
Singing to their Queen, Niente.

14 *THE PRINCESS NOBODY.*

"What have you called her?" he asked.

"Till your Majesty's return, we thought it better not to christen the Princess," said the Nurse, "so we have called her by the Italian name for *Nothing :* NIENTE; the Princess Niente, your Majesty."

When the King heard *that*, and remembered that he had promised to give NIENTE to the Dwarf, he hid his face in his hands and groaned. Nobody knew what he meant, or why he was sad, so he thought it best to keep it to himself. He went in and kissed the Queen, and comforted her, and looked at the BABY. Never was there a BABY so beautiful; she was like a Fairy's child, and so light, she could sit on a flower and not crush it. She had little wings on her back; and all the birds were fond of her. The peasants and common

THE PRINCESS NOBODY. 15

people (who said they "could not see why the *first* Royal baby should be called 'Ninety'") always spoke of her as the Princess Nobody. Only the Courtiers called her Niente. The Water Fairy was her Godmother, but (for a Fairy reason) they concealed her *real* name, and of course, she was not *christened* Niente. Here you may see her sitting teaching the little Birds to sing. They are all round her in a circle, each of them singing his very best. Great fun she and all her little companions had with the Birds; here they are, riding on them,

16   *THE PRINCESS NOBODY.*

and tumbling off when the Bird kicks. And here, again, you may observe the baby Princess riding a Parrot, while one of her Maids of Honour teases an Owl. Never was there such a happy country; all Birds and Babies, playing together, singing, and as merry as the day was long.

Well, this joyful life went on till the Princess Niente was growing quite a big girl; she was nearly fourteen. Then, one day, came a tremendous knock at the Palace gates. Out rushed the Porter, and saw a little Dwarf, in a red cap, and a red cloak, riding a green Frog.

THE PRINCESS NOBODY. 17

What a Baby: how absurd
To be bullied by a Bird!

"Tell the King he is wanted," said the Dwarf.

The Porter carried this rude message, and the King went trembling to the door.

"I have come to claim your promise; you give me NIENTE," said the Dwarf, in his froggy voice.

18   *THE PRINCESS NOBODY.*

Now the King had spoken long ago about his foolish promise, to the Queen of the Water Fairies, a very powerful person, and God-mother of his child.

"The Dwarf must be one of *my* people, if he rides a Frog," the Queen of the Water Fairies had said. "Just send him to *me*, if he is troublesome."

The King remembered this when he saw the Dwarf, so he put a bold face on it.

"That's you, is it?" said the King to the Dwarf. "Just you go to the Queen of the Water Fairies; she will have a word to say to you."

When the Dwarf heard that, it was *his* turn to tremble. He shook his little fist at the King; he half-drew his sword.

"I'll have NIENTE yet," he said, and he set spurs to his Frog, and bounded off to see the Queen of the Water Fairies.

It was night by the time the Dwarf reached the stream where the Queen lived, among the long flags and rushes and reeds of the river.

Here you see him by the river; how tired his Frog looks! He is talking to the Water Fairy. Well, he and the Water Fairy had a long talk, and the end of it was that the Fairy found only one way of

20   *THE PRINCESS NOBODY.*

saving the Princess. She flew to the king, and said, "I can only help you by making the Princess vanish clean away. I have a bird here on whose back she can fly away in safety. The Dwarf will not get her, but you will never see her again, unless a brave Prince can find her where she is hidden, and guarded by my Water Fairies."

Then the poor mother and father cried dreadfully, but they saw there was no hope. It was better that the Princess should vanish away, than that she should be married to a horrid rude Dwarf, who rode on a Frog. So they sent for the Princess, and kissed her, and embraced her, and wept over her, and (gradually she faded out of their very arms, and vanished clean away) then she flew away on the bird's back.

Here's a Dwarf upon a Snail,
Take him off at once to jail!

CHAPTER II.

IN MUSHROOM LAND.

NOW all the Kingdom next to Fairy Land was miserable, and all the people were murmuring, and the King and Queen were nearly melted in tears. They thought of all ways to recover their dear daughter, and at last the Queen hit on a plan.

"My dear," she said to the King, "let us offer to give our daughter for a wife, to any Prince who will only find her and bring her home."

"Who will want to marry a girl he can't see?" said the King. "If they have not married pretty girls they *can* see, they won't care for poor Niente."

22   *THE PRINCESS NOBODY.*

"Never mind; we can only try," said the Queen. So she sent out messengers into all the world, and sent the picture of the Princess everywhere, and proclaimed that the beautiful Princess Niente, and no less than three-quarters of the Kingdom would be given to the Prince

IN MUSHROOM LAND. 23

that could find the Princess and bring her home. And there was to
be a great tournament, or sham fight, at the Palace to amuse all the
Princes before they went on the search. So many Princes gathered
together, all full of hope; and they rode against each other with spears
and swords, and knocked each other about, and afterwards dined and
danced, and made merry. Some Fairy Knights, too, came over the
border, and they fought with spears, riding Beetles and Grasshoppers,
instead of horses. Here is a picture of a "joust," or tournament,
between two sets of Fairy Knights. By all these warlike exercises,
they increased their courage till they felt brave enough to fight all the
Ghosts, and all the Giants, if only they could save the beautiful
Princess.

24 *THE PRINCESS NOBODY.*

Well, the tournaments were over, and off all the Princes went into Fairy Land. What funny sights they saw in Fairy Land! They saw a great Snail race, the Snails running so fast, that some of the Fairy jockeys fell off on the grass. They saw a Fairy boy dancing with a Squirrel, and they found all the birds, and all the beasts, quite friendly and kind, and able to talk like other people. This was the way in old times, but now no beasts talk, and no birds, except Parrots only.

IN MUSHROOM LAND. 25

Now among all this gallant army of Princes, one was ugly, and he looked old, and odd, and the rest laughed at him, and called him the Prince Comical. But he had a kind heart. One day, when he was out walking alone, and thinking what he could do to find the Princess, he saw three bad little boys teasing a big Daddy Long Legs. They had got hold of one of his legs, and were pulling at it with all their might. When the Prince Comical saw this, he ran up and drove the bad boys away, and rubbed the limb of the Daddy Long Legs, till he gave up groaning and crying. Then the Daddy Long Legs sat up, and said in a weak voice, "You have been very kind to me; what can I do for *you?*"

"Oh, help me," said the Prince, "to find the Princess Niente! *You* fly everywhere; don't you know where she is?"

26   *THE PRINCESS NOBODY.*

"*I* don't know," said the Daddy Long Legs, mournfully. "I have never flown so far. But I know that you are all in a very dangerous part of Fairy Land. And I will take you to an aged Black Beetle, who can give you the best advice."

So saying, the Daddy Long Legs walked off with the Prince till they came to the Black Beetle.

"Can *you* tell this Prince," said the Daddy Long Legs, "where the Princess Niente is hidden?"

"I know it is in Mushroom Land," said the Beetle; "but he will want a guide."

"Will *you* be my guide?" asked the Prince.

"Yes," said the Beetle; "but what about your friends, the other Princes?"

"Oh, they must come too; it would not be fair to leave them behind," said the Prince Comical.

He was *the soul of honour;* and though the others laughed at him, he would not take advantage of his luck, and run away from them.

"Well, you *are* a true Knight," said the Black Beetle; "but before we go into the depths of Mushroom Land, just you come here with me."

Then the Black Beetle pointed out to the Prince a great smooth round red thing, a long way off.

"That is the first Mushroom in Mushroom Land," said the Beetle. "Now come with me, and you shall see, what you shall see."

So the Prince followed the Beetle, till they came to the Mushroom.

"Climb up and look over," said the Beetle.

So the Prince climbed up, and looked over. There he saw a crowned King, sound asleep.

28 *THE PRINCESS NOBODY.*

Here is the Prince Comical (you see he is not very handsome!); and here is the King so sound asleep.

"Try to waken him," said the Beetle; "just try."

So the Prince tried to waken the King, but it was of no use.

"Now, take a warning by *that*," said the Black Beetle, "and never go to sleep under a Mushroom in Mushroom country. You will never wake, if you do, till the Princess Niente is found again."

IN MUSHROOM LAND. 29

Well, the Prince Comical said he would remember that, and he and the Beetle went off and found the other Princes. They were disposed to laugh at being led by a Black Beetle; but one of them, who was very learned, reminded them that armies had been led before by Woodpeckers, and Wolves, and Humming Birds.

So they all moved on, and at night they were very tired.

Now there were no houses, and not many trees, in Mushroom Land, and when night came all the Princes wanted to lie down under a very big Mushroom.

It was in vain that the Black Beetle and Prince Comical warned them to beware.

As they marched through Mushroom Land the twilight came upon them, and
the Elves began to come out for their dance, for Elves only dance at dusk, and they

could not help joining them, which was very imprudent, as they had plenty to do the next day, and it would have been wiser if they had gone to sleep.

The Elves went on with their play till midnight, and exactly
the boughs of a big tree and went to sleep. You may wonder how th
Land, of course. But they cannot really help knowing, as it is exact
come up.

Now the Elves covered every branch of the tree, as you can see in th
decided to lie down under a very big Mushroom.

...idnight the Elves stopped their play, and undressed, and got up into

...lves know when it is midnight, as there are no clocks in Mushroom

... twelve that the Mushrooms begin to grow, and the little Mushrooms

...icture, and the Fairies did not know where to lie down. At last they

THE PRINCESS NOBODY.

"Nonsense," they said. "*You* may sleep out in the open air if you like, we mean to make ourselves comfortable here."

So they all lay down under the shelter of the Mushroom, and Prince Comical slept in the open air. In the morning he wakened, feeling very well and hungry, and off he set to call his friends. But he might as well have called the Mushroom itself. There they all lay under its shade; and though some of them had their eyes open, not one of them could move. The Prince shook them, dragged them, shouted at them, and pulled their hair. But the more he shouted and dragged, the louder they snored; and the worst of it was that he could not pull them out of the shadow of the Magic Mushroom. So there he had to leave them, sound asleep.

The Prince thought the Elves could help him perhaps, so he went and asked them how to waken his friends. They were all awake, and the Fairies were dressing the baby-Elves. But they only said, "Oh! it's their fault for sleeping under a Mushroom. Anybody would know that is a stupid thing to do. Besides, we have no time to attend to them, as the sun will be up soon, and we must get these Babies dressed and be off before then."

"Why, where are you going to?" said the Prince.

"Ah! nobody knows where we go to in the day time," said the Elves.

And nobody does.

"Well, what am I to do now?" said the Prince to the Black Beetle.

36   *THE PRINCESS NOBODY.*

"*I* don't know where the Princess is," said the Beetle; "but the Blue Bird is very wise, and *he* may know. Now your best plan will be to steal two of the Blue Bird's eggs, and not give them back till he tells you all he can."

So off they set for the Blue Bird's nest; and, to make a long story short, the Prince stole two of the eggs, and would not give them back, till the Bird promised to tell him all it knew. And the end of it was, that the Bird carried him to the Court of the Queen of Mushroom Land. She was sitting, in her crown, on a Mushroom, and she looked very funny and mischievous.

IN MUSHROOM LAND

Here you see the Prince, with his hat off, kissing the Queen's hair, and asking for the Princess.

"Oh, *she's* quite safe," said the Queen of Mushroom Land; "but what a funny boy you are. You are not *half* handsome enough for the Princess Niente."

The poor Prince blushed. "They call me Prince Comical," said he. "I know I'm not half good enough!"

"You are *good* enough for anything," said the Queen of Mushroom Land; "but you might be prettier."

Then she touched him with her wand, and he became as handsome a Prince as ever was seen, in a beautiful red silk doublet, slashed with white, and a long gold-coloured robe.

"*Now* you will do for my Princess Niente," said the Queen of Mushroc
away to the Princess Niente."

So they flew, and they flew, all day and all night, and next d
funny little people. And there, with all her long yellow hair round h
at her feet, and knelt on one knee, and asked the Princess to be his lo
Church of the Elves, and the Glowworm sent his torches, and all t
travel home, to the King and the Queen.

and. "Blue Bird" (and she whispered in the Bird's ear), "take him

hey came to a green bower, all full of Fairies, and Butterflies, and
here sat the Princess Niente. And the Prince Charming laid his Crown
nd his lady. And she did not refuse him, so they were married in the
ells of all the flowers made a merry peal. And soon they were to

Here's the Water Fairy's Court,
Nymphs and Nixies making sport!

CHAPTER III

LOST AND FOUND.

NOW the Prince had found the Princess, and you might think they had nothing to do but go home again. The father and mother of the Princess were wearying very much to hear about her. Every day they climbed to the bartizan of the Castle, and looked across the plain, hoping to see dust on the road, and some brave Prince riding back with their daughter. But she never came, and their hair grew grey with sorrow and time. The parents of the other Princes, too, who were all asleep under the Mushroom, were alarmed about their sons, and feared that they had all been taken prisoners, or perhaps eaten up by some Giant. But Princess Niente and Prince Charming were lingering in the enchanted land, too happy to leave the flowers, the brooks, and the Fairies.

The faithful Black Beetle often whispered to the Prince that it was time to turn homewards, but the Prince paid no more attention to his ally than if he had been an Ear-wig. So there, in the Valley Magical, the Prince and Princess might be wandering to this day but for a very sad accident. The night they were married, the Princess had said to the Prince, "Now you may call me Niente, or any pet name you like; but never call me by my own name."

42   *THE PRINCESS NOBODY.*

"But I don't know it," said the Prince. "Do tell me what it is?"

"Never," said the Princess; "you must never seek to know it."

"Why not?" said the Prince.

"Something dreadful will happen," said the Princess, "if ever you find out my name, and call me by it."

And she looked quite as if she could be very angry.

Now ever after this, the Prince kept wondering what his wife's real name could be, till he made himself quite unhappy.

"Is it Margaret?" he would say, when he thought the Princess was off her guard; or, "is it Joan?" "Is it Dorothy?" "It can't be Sybil, can it?"

But she would never tell him.

Now, one morning, the Princess awoke very early, but she felt so happy that she could not sleep. She lay awake and listened to the Birds singing, and then she watched a Fairy-boy teasing a Bird, which sang (so the boy said) out of tune, and another Fairy-baby riding on a Fly.

LOST AND FOUND. 43

At last the Princess, who thought the Prince was sound alseep, began to croon softly a little song she had made about him and her. She had never told him about the song, partly because she was shy, and partly for another reason. So she crooned and hummed to herself,

> *Oh, hand in hand with Gwendoline,*
> *While yet our locks are gold,*
> *He'll fare among the forests green,*
> *And through the gardens old;*
> *And when, like leaves that lose their green,*
> *Our gold has turned to grey,*
> *Then, hand in hand with Gwendoline,*
> *He'll fade and pass away!*

44   *THE PRINCESS NOBODY.*

"Oh, *Gwendoline* is your name, is it?" said the Prince, who had been wide awake, and listening to her song. And he began to laugh at having found out her secret, and tried to kiss her.

But the Princess turned very, very cold, and white like marble, so that the Prince began to shiver, and he sat down on a fallen Mushroom, and hid his face in his hands, and, in a moment, all his beautiful hair vanished, and his splendid clothes, and his gold train, and his Crown. He wore a red cap, and common clothes, and was Prince Comical once more. But the Princess arose, and she vanished swiftly away.

Opposite you see the poor Prince crying, and the Princess vanishing away. Thus he was punished for being curious and prying. It is natural, you will say, that a man should like to call his wife by her name. But the Fairies would not allow it, and, what is more, there are still some nations who will not allow a woman to mention the name of her husband.

46   *THE PRINCESS NOBODY.*

Well, here was a sad state of things! The Princess was lost as much as ever, and Prince Charming was changed back into Prince Comical. The Black Beetle sighed day and night, and mingled his tears with those of the Prince. But neither of them knew what to do. They wandered about the Valley Magical, and though it was just as pretty as ever, it seemed quite ugly and stupid to them. The worst of it was, that the Prince felt so foolish. After winning the greatest good fortune, and the dearest bride in the world, he had thrown everything away. He walked about crying, "Oh, Gwen — I mean, oh, Niente! dear Niente! return to your own Prince Comical, and all will be forgiven!"

It is impossible to say what would have happened; and probably the Prince would have died of sorrow and hunger (for he ate nothing), if the Black Beetle had not one day met a Bat, which was the favourite charger of Puck. Now Puck, as all the world knows, is the Jester at the Court of Fairy Land. He can make Oberon and Titania — the

King and Queen — laugh at the tricks he plays, and therefore they love him so much that there is nothing they would not do for him. So the Black Beetle began to talk about his master, the Prince, to the Bat Puck commonly rode; and the Bat, a good-natured creature, told the whole story to Puck. Now Puck was also in a good humour, so he jumped at once on his Bat's back, and rode off to consult the King and Queen of Fairy Land. Well, they were sorry for the Prince — he had only broken one little Fairy law after all — and they sent Puck back to tell him what he was to do. This was to find the Blue Bird again, and get the Blue Bird to guide him to the home of the Water Fairy, the Godmother of the Princess.

48   *THE PRINCESS NOBODY.*

Long and far the Prince wandered, but at last he found the Blue
Bird once more. And the Bird (very good-naturedly) promised to fly
in front of him till he led him to the beautiful stream, where the
Water Fairy held her court. So they reached it at last, and then the
Blue Bird harnessed himself to the chariot of the Water Fairy, and the
chariot was the white cup of a Water Lily. Then he pulled, and
pulled at the chariot (here he is dragging along the Water Fairy), till

he brought her where the Prince was waiting. At first, when she saw him, she was rather angry. "Why did you find out my God-daughter's name?" she said; and the Prince had no excuse to make. He only turned red, and sighed. This rather pleased the Water Fairy.

"Do you love the Princess very much?" said she.

"Oh, more than all the world," said the Prince.

"Then back you go, to Mushroom Land, and you will find her in the old place. But perhaps she will not be pleased to forgive you at first."

50   *THE PRINCESS NOBODY.*

The Prince thought he would chance *that*, but he did not say so. He only bowed very low, and thanked the Water Fairy. Then off he set, with the Blue Bird to guide him, in search of Mushroom Land. At long and at last he reached it, and glad he was to see the little sentinel on the border of the country.

LOST AND FOUND. 51

All up and down Mushroom Land the Prince searched, and at last he saw his own Princess, and he rushed up, and knelt at her feet, and held out his hands to ask pardon for having disobeyed the Fairy law.

But she was still rather cross, and down she jumped, and ran round the Mushroom, and he ran after her.

So he chased her for a minute or two, and at last she laughed, and popped up her head over the Mushroom, and pursed up her lips into a cherry. And he kissed her across the Mushroom, and knew he had won back his own dear Princess, and they felt even happier than if they had never been parted.

"Journeys end in lovers meeting," and so do Stories. The Prince has his Princess once again, and I can tell you they did not wait long, this time, in the Valley Magical. Off they went, straight home, and the Black Beetle guided them, flying in a bee-line. Just on the further border of Mushroom Land, they came to all the Princes fast asleep. But when the Princess drew near, they all wakened, and jumped up,

and they slapped the fortunate Prince on the back, and wished him luck, and cried, "Hullo, Comical, old chap; we hardly knew you! Why, you've grown quite handsome!" And so he had; he was changed into Prince Charming again, but he was so happy he never noticed it, for he was not conceited. But the Princess noticed it, and she loved him all the better. Then they all made a procession, with the Black Beetle marching at the head; indeed, they called him "Black Rod" now, and he was quite a Courtier.

So with flags flying, and music playing, they returned to the home of the Princess. And the King and Queen met them at the park gates, and fell on the neck of the Prince and Princess, and kissed

54   *THE PRINCESS NOBODY.*

them, and laughed, and cried for joy, and kissed them again. You may be sure the old Nurse was out among the foremost, her face quite shining with pleasure, and using longer words than the noblest there. And she admired the Prince very much, and was delighted that "her girl," as she called the Princess, had got such a good husband. So here we leave them, and that country remained always happy, and so it has neither history nor geography. Therefore you won't find it on any map, nor can you read about it in any book but this book.

As to the Black Beetle, he was appointed to a place about the Court, but he never married, he had no children, and there are no *other* Black Beetles, consequently, in the country where the Prince and Princess became King and Queen.

LOST AND FOUND. 55

ERANT OLIM REX QUIDAM ET REGINA.

Apulieus.

Au Temps jadis! as Perrault says,
In half-forgotten Fairy days, —
"There lived a King once, and a Queen,
As few there are, as more have been," —
Ah, still we love the well-worn phrase,
Still love to tread the ancient ways,
To break the fence, to thread the maze,
To see the beauty we have seen,
        Au Temps jadis!

Here's luck to every child that strays
In Fairy Land among the Fays;
That follows through the forest green
Prince Comical and Gwendoline;
That reads the tales we used to praise,
        Au Temps jadis!

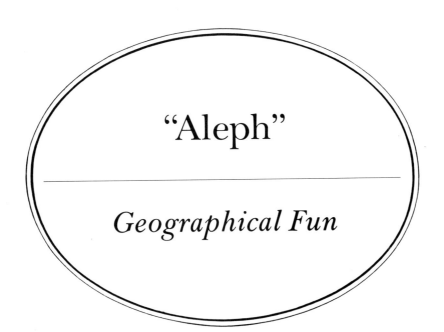

"Aleph"

Geographical Fun

ENGLAND.

Vincent Brooks, Day & Son, Lith. London, W.C.

Beautiful England,—on her Island throne,—
Grandly she rules,—with half the world her own ;

From her vast empire the sun ne'er departs :
She reigns a Queen—Victoria, Queen of Hearts.

SCOTLAND.

A gallant piper, struggling through the bogs,
His wind bag broken, wearing his clay clogs;

Yet, strong of heart, a fitting emblem makes
For Scotland—land of heroes and of cakes.

WALES.

Geography bewitch'd—Owen Glendowr,
In Bardic grandeur, looks from shore to shore,
And sings King Arthur's long, long pedigree,
And cheese and leeks, and knights of high degree.

IRELAND.

And what shall typify the Emerald Isle?
A Peasant, happy in her baby's smile?

No fortune her's,—though rich in native grace,—
Herrings, potatoes, and a joyous face.

SPAIN & PORTUGAL.

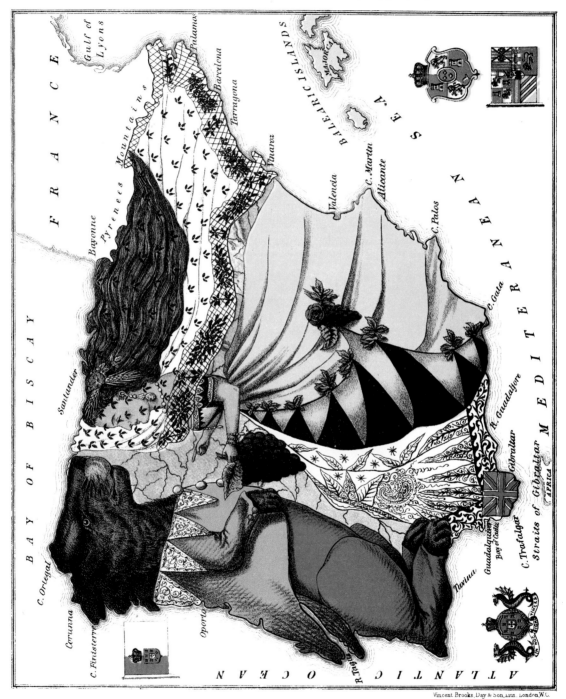

These long divided nations soon may be,
By Prims' grace, joined in lasting amity.

And ladies fair—if King Fernando rules,
Grow grapes in peace, and fatten their pet mules.

Vincent Brooks, Day & Son, Lith. London, W.C.

FRANCE.

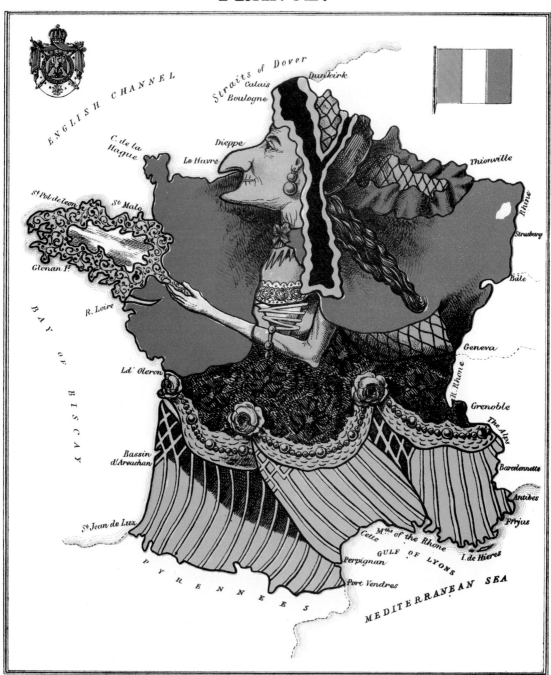

Vincent Brooks, Day & Son, Lith. London, W.C.

A hook-nosed lady represents fair France,
Empress of cooks, of fashions, and the dance.

Her flatt'ring glass declares that vict'ry, power,
Beauty, wealth, arts, are her imperial dower.

ITALY.

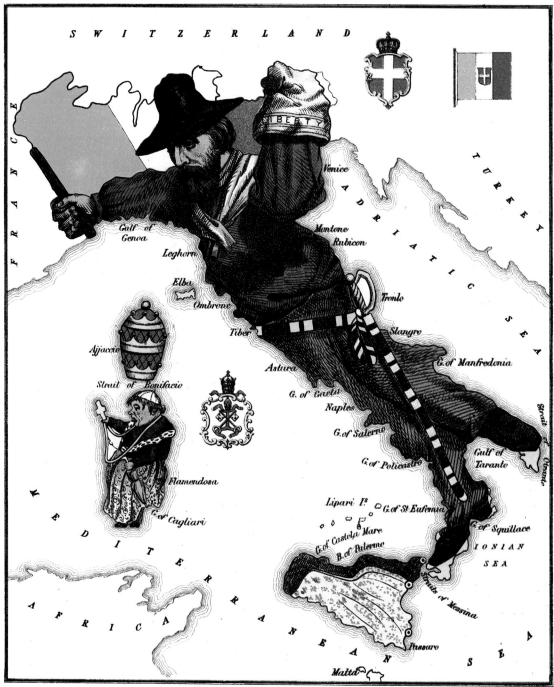

Vincent Brooks, Day & Son, Lith. London, W.C.

Thou model chieftain—born in modern days—
Well may thy gallant acts claim classic praise.

Uncompromising friend of liberty!
Thy Photograph ennobles Italy!

PRUSSIA.

Vincent Brooks, Day & Son, Lith. London.W.C

His Majesty of Prussia—grim and old—
Sadowa's King—by needle guns made bold ;

With Bismark of the royal conscience, keeper,
In dreams political none wiser—deeper.

170

GERMANY.

Lo! studious Germany, in her delight,
At coming glories, shewn by second sight,

And on her visioned future proudly glancing,
Her joy expresses by a lady dancing.

HOLLAND AND BELGIUM.

Dame Holland, trick'd out in her gala clothes,
And Master Belgium, with a punchy nose;

Seem on the map to represent a land,
By patriot worth, and perfect art made grand.

DENMARK.

For Shakespeare's Prince, and the Princess of Wales,
To England dear. Her royal spirit quails;

From skating faint, she rests upon the snow;
Shrinking from unclean beasts that grin below.

RUSSIA.

Peter, and Catherine, and Alexander,
Mad Paul, and Nicholas, poor shadows wander

Out in the cold; while **Emperor A. the Second**
In Eagles, Priests, and Bears supreme is reckoned.

R. M. Ballantyne

The Butterfly's Ball

Come, take up your hats, and
away let us haste
To the Butterfly's ball and the Grass-
hopper's feast;
The trumpeter Gad-fly has summon'd the crew,
And the revels are now only waiting for you.
On the smooth-shaven grass by the side of the wood,
Beneath a broad oak that for ages has stood,
See the children of earth, and the tenants of air,
For an evening's amusement together repair.

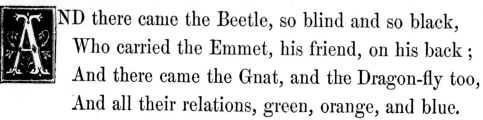

ND there came the Beetle, so blind and so black,
Who carried the Emmet, his friend, on his back;
And there came the Gnat, and the Dragon-fly too,
And all their relations, green, orange, and blue.

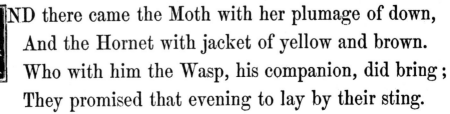

ND there came the Moth with her plumage of down,
And the Hornet with jacket of yellow and brown.
Who with him the Wasp, his companion, did bring;
They promised that evening to lay by their sting.

HEN the sly little Dormouse peep'd out of
his hole,
And led to the feast his blind cousin the
Mole;

AND the Snail, with her horns peeping out from
  her shell,
Came fatigued with the distance, the length
  of an ell.

 MUSHROOM the table, and on it were spread
A Water-dock-leaf, which their table-cloth made ;
The viands were various, to each of their taste,
And the Bee brought the honey to sweeten the feast.

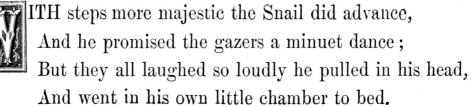

ITH steps more majestic the Snail did advance,
And he promised the gazers a minuet dance;
But they all laughed so loudly he pulled in his head,
And went in his own little chamber to bed.

HEN, as evening gave way to the shadows of night,
Their watchman, the Glow-worm, came out with his light:
So home let us hasten, while yet we can see,
For no watchman is waiting for you or for me.